HONEY COOKERY

Energizing and mineral-rich honey is the ideal substance for cookery. This book contains over 150 recipes for meat and fish dishes, salads, soups, *hors d'oeuvre* and sweet courses, all featuring honey as an ingredient.

GW00702875

HONEY COOKERY

by
CHRIS STADTLAENDER

Translated from the German
by
JANET A. YOUNG

NATURE'S WAY

THORSONS PUBLISHERS LIMITED
Wellingborough, Northamptonshire

First published in Germany as Kocke mit honig
koche gesund by Chris Stadtlaender
© Mary Hahns Kochbuchverlag, Berlin 30, 1965
First English edition 1967
Second (paperback) edition 1972
Second Impression 1976
Third Impression 1977
Fourth Impression 1978

ISBN 0 7225 0199 4

Made and Printed in Great Britain by
Weatherby Woolnough, Wellingborough
Northants, England, NN8 4BX

PREFACE

Honey, produced by countless bees from nectar obtained from thousands of blooms is, without doubt, one of the most valuable and beneficial of foods.

Its value was recognised by the people of former times. Moreover, they regarded it not only as a food but as a medicine. The following is a recipe from ancient Athens, inscribed on wax tablets about 100 B.C.; "*'FIG DISH'*: Mix boiled pig fat and thick groats with milk. Blend this mixture into fresh cheese, add egg-yolks and brains. Cover this with a fragrant fig leaf and cook in a broth of poultry or goat's meat. When cooked, take it out of the pot, remove fig leaf and place the mixture in a vessel full of boiling honey. When it has become sufficiently yellow, serve it either with the boiled honey or another honey."

This may not sound very palatable but it serves to indicate that our ancestors made greater use of this wonderful commodity than most of us do today.

In 400 B.C. the great doctor Hippocrates recommended honey as a means of curing ulcers, and we know that it also purifies festering and dirty wounds by its power of extraction.

The Songs of Solomon in the Bible, has this to say:

"Eat honey my son for it is good and virgin honey is sweet in your mouth."

The Roman poet Virgil wrote in his "Georgics":

"Many a man led by such proffs and such examples accepted that a part of the Holy Spirit and ethereal breath lived in the bees."

Unfortunately, most housewives are unaware how advantageously honey can be used in cookery and usually one only sees it on the breakfast table when even then it is quite often rejected in favour of marmalade or some other preserve. On the other hand, it is well known as an authentic treatment for colds when taken with hot milk or lemon.

This book, above all, fulfils the purpose of showing the housewife the many different ways of using honey. It is not so strange as it may seem to serve honey as a garnish for meat and fish dishes or to serve a vegetable soup with it. For honey has a very individual quality as a spice: it emphasises the individual taste of each dish, enriching the dish as a whole, without being overpowering. We need not be afraid, therefore, of giving our imagination free rein in the kitchen when we are using honey.

Honey provides the right kind of moist texture in gingerbread, as it is hygroscopic,* which prevents the gingerbread drying up. Syrup or molasses do not possess this precious quality.

Finally, honey is necessary as an active ingredient in selected foods.

* Capable of absorbing moisture.

CONTENTS

INTRODUCTION

Honey is tasty, nourishing and beneficial

Bees collect honey as a supply for the winter. Honey is made in such a way that it is a complete food for the bees, who have no need of further nourishment. For human beings, too, honey is an excellent form of nourishment, for it contains substances important for a healthy life. It consists mainly of fruit and grape sugar—also called invert sugar—which can be readily assimilated by the body and used as a quick-acting energiser. It also contains power enzymes, which separate the sugars, aromatic substances, minerals and hormones. In this category are the "controlling" substances, which stop the growth of certain bacteria.

The industrious bees are responsible for producing a most tasty food for healthy people and yet mild and beneficent for sick people. Honey strengthens children and is splendid for adults too, especially for those involved in energetic activities.

Honey has a favourable effect on the heart and the circulation of the blood and is helpful in the relief of colds. It can eliminate poisons and can be used for healing certain liver, stomach and intestinal diseases. As it contains no salt, it is of particular benefit in certain illnesses.

Advice for the housewife when buying honey

The various colours are a result of the different blooms from which the bees have collected the honey. For example, honey from the lime tree or the acacia is pale or light, while that from heather is yellowy-brown and honey from woodland trees or firs is dark brown.

The fact that honey is either thick or clear is readily explained. Honey, in its natural state, at some stage becomes firm, some kinds more quickly than others—this is dependent on the amount of grape sugar contained. It must be understood that, whether honey in its natural state is firm or runny, its nutritional value is the same, and that honey which has become firm can easily be turned into a liquid by placing it in warm water for an appropriate period. (The water should not be hotter than 50°C, 122°F, so that it is not too hot for the hand.) The nutritional value is the same as before and after heating; in the same way that ice and water are the same. They only differ as regards consistency.

How to conserve honey correctly

This is quite simple. Store your jars in a dark, cool, and dry place and protect the contents from damp and any strong smelling foods—then you will enjoy eating your honey and the many recipes in this little book, using honey to the greatest benefit, will be completely at your disposal.

SALADS

CHAPTER I

SALADS

Swiss Cheese Salad

1 lb Assorted Cheeses	Caraway Seeds
2 teaspoonsful Oil	⎧ Pickled Cucumbers
1 tablespoonful Lemon	⎪ Lettuce
Juice	4 oz. ⎨ Bitter-sweet Paprika
1 tablespoonful Cream	⎪ Cocktail Onions
1 tablespoonful Mustard	⎩ Mushrooms
1 teaspoonful Honey	Pinch of Salt
Few drops Chili Sauce	Pinch of Cayenne Pepper

Cut the cheese into small squares. Mix together the
pickled cucumbers, lettuce soaked in oil, bitter-
sweet paprika, cocktail onions and ·mushrooms.
Beat together the oil, lemon juice, cream, mustard,
HONEY, chili sauce, salt, cayenne pepper and
caraway seeds to form a sauce and pour over the
salad. Leave to stand for one hour.

Florentine Sauerkraut Salad

2 sliced Apples	1 small bunch Grapes
⅛ pint Sweet Cream	(Cherries or other fresh
2 tablespoonsful Honey	fruit can also be used)
1 tablespoonful Mustard	14 oz. fresh chopped
	Sauerkraut

Mix well together the apples, grapes, cream,
HONEY, and mustard. Add the freshly chopped
sauerkraut and decorate with grapes and nuts.

Coconut and Fruit Salad

1 Coconut   Mixture of: Strawberries, Gooseberries,
        Red Currants, Blackcurrants
        Honey to sweeten

After washing, sprinkle the mixture of fresh berries with HONEY. Mix them with the grated pulp of a coconut and fill the empty shell with this mixture. Place on ice and serve cold.

Orange Salad

1 small firm Cabbage	1 cooking Apple
1 large Orange	1 tablespoonful Wine Vinegar
1 tablespoonful Lemon Juice	3 tablespoonsful Olive Oil
1 teaspoonful Honey	Pinch Sea Salt and White Pepper

Cut the cabbage and apple into slices. Cut the orange into pieces and mix together. Beat up the wine vinegar, lemon juice, olive oil and HONEY to form a sauce, and flavour with the salt and pepper. Pour over the apple and cabbage.

Chinese Apple Salad

12 oz. cooking Apples	Juice of an Orange
4 teaspoonsful Honey	Grated rind of an Orange
Dash of Brandy	Candied Cherries, Sultanas and grated Walnuts

Peel the apples and slice thinly. Mix the orange juice and peel with the HONEY and brandy and pour over the apples. Garnish with the cherries, sultanas and walnuts.

'Mignon' Fruit Salad

5 ripe Blue Plums	2 Oranges
3 Apples	4 oz. Yellow Plums
1 Egg Yolk	4 oz. Walnuts
1 glass Light White Wine	2 teaspoonsful Honey
Pistachio Nuts and Cherries	Sugar to taste

Divide plums, oranges, apples, and walnuts into small pieces, and arrange in layers in a glass dish. Pour sugar over fruit. Mix the wine, egg yolk, HONEY, and thicken by placing in a bowl of hot water over a gentle heat. When it has cooled pour it among the fruit and decorate with candied pistachio nuts and cherries.

'Hawaiian' Poultry Salad

1 cooked Chicken	4 slices tinned Pineapple
1 Banana	1 cooking Apple
1 small tin Mushrooms	Capers
1 cup Mayonnaise	6 teaspoonsful Orange Juice
6 teaspoonsful Grapefruit Juice	3 teaspoonsful Honey
Pinch Chili Sauce, Salt, Red Pepper	1 Tomato

Separate the cooked chicken into pieces. Chop up the pineapple, and cut the banana and cooking apple into thin slices, and add to the tin of mushrooms. Mix well together with a few capers. Beat the mayonnaise with the orange juice, grapefruit juice and HONEY and season with the chili sauce, salt and pepper, and add the centre of the tomato. Pour the sauce over the chicken, pineapple, banana, apple and mushrooms, and serve cold.

The Chef's Fruit Salad

3 Oranges	1 Lemon
4 Figs	2 Bananas
4 Dates	2½ oz. Nuts
2 Apples (medium size)	3 teaspoonsful liquid
2½ oz. Sultanas	Honey
1 liqueur glass Rum	Juice of half Lemon

Cut up the oranges, lemons, figs, dates, bananas, apples, and nuts into thin slices. Soak the sultanas in hot water and drain. Place the sliced fruit and nuts with the sultanas in a glass bowl, and add HONEY. Mix the rum with the lemon juice and add to the mixture. Serve cold.

Fine White Cabbage Salad

9 oz. White Cabbage	Olive Oil
1 cooking Apple	2 tablespoonsful Lemon
½ coffeespoonful of	Juice
Caraway Seeds	4 crushed Juniper Berries
½ teaspoonful grated Onion	Pinch Pepper and Salt
2 oz. Raisins	2 oz. chopped Walnuts
2 tablespoonsful Honey	

Finely grate the cabbage and crush in olive oil and leave to stand for several hours. Add the grated cooking apple, lemon juice, caraway seeds, juniper berries, onion and salt and pepper. Mix well and before serving mix in the raisins and walnuts with the HONEY.

16

Fruit Salad

2 ripe Pears
2 Bananas
Handful Cashew Nuts
Small glass Kirsch
1 teaspoonful Vanilla Sugar

2 Apricots
1 Apple
2 tablespoonsful Honey
Pinch Cinnamon
½ cup Fruit Juice

Peel and skin the pears, apricots, bananas and apple and cut into sections. Chop the cashew nuts and mix with the fruit. Whisk the HONEY, kirsch, cinnamon and vanilla sugar with the fruit juice until it forms a sauce. Pour over the fruit and serve cold.

'Cap Ferrat' Salad

5 oz. cooked Chicken
6 Sardines
1 cooked Carrot
3 boiled Eggs
½ cooked Celery head
2 teaspoonsful Mustard
  Powder
3 tablespoonsful Wine
  Vinegar
Salt, Chili Sauce, Black
  Pepper

1 Lettuce
3½ oz. raw Ham
3 boiled Potatoes
2 ripe Apples
1 Cabbage heart
2 Green Tomatoes
1 teaspoonful Honey
4 tablespoonsful Salad Oil
1 teaspoonful Cocktail
  Onions

Cut the chicken, ham, sardines, potatoes, carrot, apples, egg whites, cabbage heart, celery, and tomatoes into small pieces and mix well together. Beat up the mustard powder with the HONEY, and add the wine vinegar, salad oil, salt, and a few drops of chili sauce, black pepper and onions and mix with the salad. Serve on a flat dish on lettuce leaves and pour beaten egg yolk over the salad.

Spiced Chicory Salad

2 firm heads of Chicory
1 teaspoonful Honey
Lemon Juice, Salt and
  Black Pepper

1 glass Yogurt
1 Tomato

Cut the chicory into thin slices. Whip up the yogurt with the HONEY and add the centre of tomato, lemon juice, salt and pepper to season. Pour the mixture over the chicory.

'Budapest' Calf's Foot Salad

1 cooked Calf's Foot
1 tablespoonful
  Mayonnaise
1 tablespoonful Honey
½ jar Yogurt
Sardines, hard boiled Eggs,
  Red Peppers and Parsley

1 Egg Yolk
1 tablespoonful Tomato
  Pulp
1 tablespoonful Mustard
Salt and Paprika

Cut the calf's foot into strips and place in a marinade of vinegar and oil. Sprinkle with paprika and leave to stand for two hours. Beat up the egg yolk, mayonnaise, tomato pulp, HONEY, mustard, yogurt, with a pinch of salt and paprika to form a sauce. Pour over the calf's foot and garnish with the sardines, hard-boiled eggs, peppers, and parsley.

'Exclusive' Shrimp Salad

1 tin Shrimps (or Crab)
2 tablespoonsful Green Peas
Cauliflower
2 raw Egg Yolks
½ tablespoonful Honey
Pinch Salt, Black Pepper

4 tablespoonsful Asparagus Tips
3 tablespoonsful chopped Mushrooms
1 cup Olive Oil
1 tablespoonful Lemon Juice
Dill, Parsley, Chervil, Chives

Mix the tin of shrimps with the asparagus tips, peas, chopped mushrooms, and an equal amount of small pieces of cauliflower. Beat up the olive oil, egg yolks, lemon juice, HONEY and spice with the dill, parsley, chervil, and chives. Add a pinch of salt and black pepper to the sauce and pour over the salad.

Housewives' Chicory Salad

2 (or more) heads of Chicory
1 tablespoonful Wine Vinegar
1 teaspoonful Honey

1 Onion
2 tablespoonsful Olive Oil
1 tablespoonful Lemon Juice
Pinch of Sugar and Salt

Wash the chicory and cut into fine slices. Prepare the sauce from the olive oil, wine vinegar, lemon juice, HONEY, and add the finely chopped onion with a pinch of sugar and salt. Pour the sauce over the salad and mix well.

Fresh Vegetable Salad from Munich

4 Cabbage hearts
2 Tomatoes
1 cup Mayonnaise
2 teaspoonsful Honey
Pepper, Red Pepper, Salt
1 Pepper

1 fresh Cucumber
4 tablespoonsful Sour Cream
2 teaspoonsful Tomato Ketchup
Juice of one Lemon

Separate the cabbage hearts into pieces. Slice the pepper, tomatoes and cucumber. Beat up the mayonnaise with the sour cream, HONEY, tomato ketchup, white and red pepper, salt, and the juice of the lemon. Pour over the cabbage and serve cold.

Hungarian 'Csalla mary' Salad

1 White Cabbage
2 Tomatoes
1 pickled Cucumber
1 Onion
2 tablespoonsful Vinegar
9 tablespoonsful Olive Oil

1 Red Pepper
1 Green Pepper
1 fresh Cucumber
2 tablespoonsful Lemon Juice
2 tablespoonsful Honey
Salt

Finely grate the cabbage, peppers, tomatoes, cucumbers and onion and mix well. Prepare a sauce from the lemon juice, vinegar, HONEY, olive oil and salt and mix with the salad.

Celery and Banana Salad

1 young head Celery
1 Banana
1 tablespoonful Honey

1 tablespoonful Lemon Juice
2 tablespoonsful Sweet
   Cream
Chopped Walnuts

Clean, peel, and grate the head of celery and add the lemon juice. Mash the banana and mix with the celery. Beat up the cream with the HONEY and add to the celery mixture. Decorate with chopped walnuts.

SAUCES AND SOUPS

CHAPTER II

SAUCES

'Calabrian' Cherry Sauce

1¾ lb. Morello Cherries	6 oz. Sugar
3 Cloves	Cinnamon, Lemon Peel
¼ pint Red Wine	1 oz. Potato Flour*
1-2 oz. Butter	Water
2 teaspoonsful Honey	1 cup of Red Wine

Gently cook the stoned cherries with the sugar, a pinch of cinnamon, piece of lemon peel, cloves and the red wine. Add the potato flour to the hot melted butter, then add the cherries, the cup of red wine and an egg-cupful of water—season with the HONEY and bring to the boil. This can be served with the dessert dishes or beef, and even with game.

Spring Sauce

½ cupful Yogurt	1 teaspoonful Honey
½ teaspoonful Lemon Juice	1 Egg Yolk
1 tablespoonful Oil	Sea Salt, Pepper
Chopped Green Vegetables	

Mix well together the yogurt, HONEY, lemon juice, egg yolk, oil, and salt and pepper (a pinch of each) and add plenty of green vegetables.

* See Appendix.

'Bombay' Honey Sauce

1 tablespoonful Honey
6 teaspoonsful Lemon
  Juice

½ teaspoonful Ground Nuts

1 Egg Yolk
¾ cupful Olive Oil
Chili Sauce, Black Pepper
  and Salt
Soaked Raisins

Mix together the HONEY, egg yolk, lemon juice, olive oil, ground nuts, a few drops of chili sauce, a pinch of black pepper and salt and beat vigorously. Whip up the curds and some soaked raisins and add to the mixture. Serve with salads or as a sauce for dipping.

Swiss Sauce

4 ripe cooking Apples
1 tablespoonful Potato
  Flour*
1 tablespoonful Honey
Juice of half a Lemon

1 oz. Butter
1 cupful White Wine
Grated Lemon Peel
Pinch Sea Salt
2 tablespoonsful Sour
  Cream

Peel the cooking apples, cut into thin slices and gently stew in the butter. Sprinkle with the potato flour and add the white wine. Then add the lemon peel, HONEY, lemon juice and sea salt. Quickly beat in the sour cream. This sauce is suitable for puddings or rice.

* See Appendix.

Brazilian Cucumber Cream

1 fresh Cucumber	2 springs Parsley
1 glass Yogurt	2 teaspoonsful Honey
½ teaspoonful Sea Salt and Black Pepper	Crushed Garlic

Wash the cucumber, dry and cut into very thin slices including the peel. Let them stand for several minutes in salt water and dry well. Chop the parsley. Empty the glass of ice-cold yogurt into a dish and add the HONEY, cucumber slices, parsley, a touch of crushed garlic, salt and pepper. Beat the mixture to a smooth cream with a wooden spoon and serve ice-cold with toast or chips.

Spicy Olive Sauce

10 green stoned Olives	Sherry
½ pint White Wine	Diced Bacon
Assorted Herbs	1 tablespoonful Tomato Pulp
Salt and Red Pepper	
½ teaspoonful Mustard	1 tablespoonful Honey

Cut the olives into quarters and cook with a little sherry. Fry the diced bacon with the chopped assorted herbs in dripping with the white wine. Add the pulped centre of tomato, olives, salt and red pepper. Mix the HONEY with the mustard, and add to the olives.

Polish Honey Sauce

2½ oz. shelled Almonds
2½ oz. Currants
¼ coffeespoonful Cinnamon
½ pint Red Wine
1 oz. Butter
¾ oz. Breadcrumbs

2½ oz. Raisins
4 Cloves
½ coffeespoonful **grated**
   Lemon Peel
1 tablespoonful Sugar
1 oz. wholewheat Flour
2 teaspoonsful Honey

Boil the shelled almonds, raisins, currants, cloves, cinnamon, grated lemon peel, with the red wine until the raisins have swollen. Cook the sugar in the butter until golden-brown. Add the flour and breadcrumbs, and mix well together with the HONEY and bring to the boil. Serve with tongue or beef.

Creamed Horse-radish with Honey

1 tablespoonful Honey
5 tablespoonsful grated
   Horse-radish

½ pint Sweet Cream
1 cooking Apple

Beat up the HONEY with the cream, and then add the horse-radish. Grate the apple and add this to the mixture. Freeze in the refrigerator before serving.

CHAPTER III

SOUPS

Buttermilk Soup

2 Egg Yolks	3 tablespoonsful Wheat
¼ pint Sweet Cream	Flour
4 tablespoonsful Honey	1¾ pints Buttermilk
Roasted Breadcrumbs	Vanilla Essence
	Pinch Salt

Beat up the egg yolks with the wheat flour and
sweet cream. Pour into the hot buttermilk and
bring to the boil under constant heat. Then stir in
the HONEY, some vanilla essence and a pinch of
salt. Serve with roasted breadcrumbs.

Grape Soup

1 heaped soup plate Grapes	2¾ pints Water
3 tablespoonsful Sugar	2 tablespoonsful Honey
1 tablespoonful Potato	2 Egg Yolks
Flour	

Remove a third of the grapes from the soup plate,
and cut the remainder into small pieces and boil
for thirty minutes in the water. Pour this soup
through a sieve and season with the sugar and
HONEY. Beat together the potato flour and egg
yolks and thicken the soup with this mixture.
Gently stew the remainder of the grapes and add
shortly before serving.

Honey-milk Soup

1¾ pints Milk
Lemon Peel
Salt
2 Egg Yolks
Soaked Raisins

1 pint Water
Pinch Cinnamon
5 tablespoonsful Semolina
3 tablespoonsful Honey

Boil the milk with just under the pint of water,
the lemon juice and pinch of cinnamon and salt.
Stir in the semolina and leave for ten minutes.
Beat up the egg yolks with the HONEY and add the
soaked raisins to the cooled soup.

Indian Apple Soup

1¼ lb. ripe apples
2 tablespoonsful Potato
    Flour
1 tablespoonful Honey
Anise

1¾ pints Water
1 cupful White Wine
3 tablespoonsful Sugar
Crumbled Biscuits

Core and remove the stalks from the ripe apples
and gently cook in the water, then pour through a
sieve. Beat up the potato flour* with the wine and
mix together to form a soup. Pour the HONEY,
sugar and a drop of anise into the cooled soup, and
serve with crumbled biscuits.

'Kiel' Malt Soup

2 oz. Honey
3½ oz. Malt extract

2 cupfuls Full Cream Milk
2 cupfuls Water

Stir the HONEY into the milk, then add the malt
extract and water. (Cook over moderate heat and
serve still hot.)

* See Appendix.

30

VEGETABLES

CHAPTER IV

VEGETABLES

Honey Vegetables and Fruit

Place in thin runny HONEY peeled cut vegetables
and fruit such as cucumbers, tomatoes, aubergines,
avocados, oranges, strawberries or melons, according to taste. Add a little chili sauce. Serve with
rice, meat or fish. The fruit or vegetable must
always be covered by the HONEY.

Lausanne Asparagus Pudding

1 lb. 2 oz. fresh Asparagus	½ pint Cream
5 oz. Flour	2 tablespoonsful Honey
1 tablespoonful Lemon	2 oz. Butter
Juice	7 oz. finely cut Ham
6 Eggs	Grated Parmesan

Gently cook the asparagus, cut into small pieces
and dry. Form a dough with the cream, flour,
HONEY, lemon juice, butter, eggs, and finely cut
ham. Roll out, and place the pastry in layers with
the asparagus in a well greased fire-proof dish.
Finish with a layer of asparagus. Cover with knobs
of butter and pour on some of the beaten egg
which has been mixed with grated parmesan.
Cook for one hour in a moderate oven.

Avocado with Fruit

1 Avocado Pear
Vanilla Essence
Cherries or strawberries

3 teaspoonsful Honey
Pinch of Sugar

Peel the pear and pass the pulp through a sieve.
Mix with the HONEY some vanilla essence and a
pinch of sugar. Arrange in layers in the shell of
the avocado and decorate with fresh cherries or
strawberries. Serve cold

Roasted Fennel Dish

3 Fennel Leaves
Curry Powder
6 tablespoonsful Cream
1 teaspoonful Honey
1 teaspoonful Parmesan
Knobs of Butter
Sea Salt

3 Tomatoes
1 Egg Yolk
1 tablespoonful
 Breadcrumbs
Pinch of Salt and Pepper
Tomato Sauce

Halve the fennel leaves, wash and gently boil in
salt water. Sprinkle with the salt and curry powder.
Cut the tomatoes into slices and add the halved
fennels. Layer in a greased soufflé dish. Add egg
milk which is made by beating up the cream, egg
yolk, HONEY, breadcrumbs, parmesan and salt and
pepper. Add knobs of butter and bake in a hot
oven for thirty minutes. Add tomato sauce.

Onions with Honey Sauce

Several medium sized   Water and Wine
    Onions
For the sauce:
1 coffeespoonful Honey   Lemon Juice
Marjoram   Pinch of Pepper

Remove the skin from the onions and cook in a
mixture of half water and half wine. Then take out
and keep warm. Make the sauce as follows: mix a
trace of marjoram with the pinch of pepper, HONEY
and a little lemon juice with the liquid drained
from the onions, so that the sauce is of a smooth
consistency. Quarter the onions and cover with
the sauce.

Beans Baked with Honey

2 cupfuls dried Haricot   1 cupful quartered Tomatoes
    Beans   ½ cupful Honey
1 teaspoonful French   3-4 diced slices Fat Bacon
    Mustard   Olive Oil
Sodium Bicarbonate   Tomato Sauce

Mix the cooked dried haricot beans with the
quartered tomato. Add the chopped-up onions,
HONEY, mustard, bacon and a touch of sodium
bicarbonate. Place everything in a well greased
casserole, pour olive oil on the beans and cook for
3-4 hours in a moderate oven. Serve with tomato
sauce.

Genoese Chestnut Hot Pot

2 lb. ripe Pears	½ lb. sweet Chestnuts
1 cupful Milk	2 tablespoonsful Honey
2 teaspoonsful Wheat Flour	4 Cloves
1 stalk Cinnamon	2½ oz. diced Fried Bacon

Quarter the pears and gently boil with a little water. Add the cinnamon and the cloves. Boil the chestnuts in salt water, remove the skins and then cook gently. Beat up the milk, flour and HONEY and mix in with the pears and chestnuts. Add the bacon to the hot pot, and cook everything gently together until soft.

Florentine Spinach with Egg and Honey Slices

1 lb. 2 oz. Spinach	1 cupful Cream
4 Egg Yolks	1 teaspoonful Honey
3 oz. grated Parmesan	4 Egg Whites

Honey Slices:	
1 cupful Milk	2 tablespoonsful Honey
White Bread	1 Egg Yolk
Salt and Pepper	

Prepare the spinach, gently cook and well drain. Whip the cream with the four egg yolks, HONEY, pinch of salt, grated parmesan cheese, and mix with the spinach. Stiffly beat the four egg whites and mix in also. Bake in a greased soufflé dish for thirty minutes. Dip thick slices of white bread in egg-milk made from one egg yolk, milk, HONEY, and a pinch of salt and pepper which has been well mixed. Fry on both sides in hot fat until golden brown.

Carrots with Honey-Nut Sauce

1 lb. 2 oz. Carrots
1 tablespoonful Flour
2 knobs Butter
1 teaspoonful Honey
Pinch of Salt

1 oz. Butter
½ pint Milk
3 tablespoonsful grated
   Hazel and Walnuts

Gently stew the young cleaned carrots in the butter and a little water over a gentle heat. Sprinkle with the flour and cover with milk. Before serving mix the knobs of butter with the grated nuts and HONEY and add to the carrots. Flavour with a pinch of salt.

Bacon Potatoes with Honey

2 oz. Wheat Flour
3½ oz. finely chopped Bacon
1 tablespoonful Honey
Salt, Cayenne Pepper,
   Curry powder

1 oz. Butter
2 tablespoonsful Mustard
1 glass Red Wine
1 cupful Sweet Cream
Boiled Potatoes

Skin and slice some boiled potatoes. Prepare a dark sauce with the wheat flour and butter. Cover with stock and add the finely chopped bacon. Mix the mustard with the HONEY and add the glass of wine and then season with the salt, cayenne pepper and a touch of curry powder. Pour the sauce over the potatoes and heat together. Add the cupful of sweet cream and serve.

'Lüneburg' Pear Dumpling Hot Pot

1 lb. 2 oz. Pears	5 cupfuls Water
1 stick Cinnamon	2 Cloves
2 tablespoonsful Sugar	9 oz. Semolina
Milk, Butter and Salt	3 teaspoonsful Potato Flour
2 tablespoonsful Honey	Streaky Bacon
2 Eggs	

Gently cook the quartered pears in the water with the cinnamon, cloves and sugar. Prepare the dumplings in the following way: Sprinkle the semolina in boiling milk, add the knob of butter and pinch of salt. Beat up the eggs with two table-spoonsful of milk and add the thick mixture, which must be cold. Form dumplings from the cold semolina. Cook in boiling salt water until they float on the surface. Thicken the pear juice with the potato flour* and add the HONEY. Cut some streaky bacon into thin pieces and fry in the pan. Add to the pears and dumplings.

Brussels Sprouts

1 lb. 2 oz. Sprouts	1½ oz. Butter
2 tablespoonsful Honey	Pinch of Salt and Nutmeg

Prepare the sprouts and steam gently. Melt the butter in a pan and toss the sprouts in the fat. Add the HONEY, salt and nutmeg and serve.

* See Appendix.

Vegetables for the Gourmet

9 oz. Asparagus Tips
9 oz. young Carrots
1 Egg Yolk
1 cupful Sweet Cream
Lettuce Leaves and Nuts

9 oz. young Peas
9 oz. young Onions
1 tablespoonful Honey
Chili Sauce, Salt, Cayenne
Pepper

Place the asparagus, peas, carrots and onions in boiling salt water and steam gently. Beat the egg yolk with HONEY, and add the cupful of cream, flavoured with the chili sauce, salt and cayenne pepper. Serve the vegetables individually on a dish, add the sauce and decorate with nuts and lettuce leaves.

Turnips in Honey Sauce

1lb. 2 oz. Turnips
½ oz. Sugar
Chopped lovage
Potato Flour*

1 pint boiling Water
Pinch of Salt
2 tablespoonsful Honey

Clean the turnips and cook in butter and sugar until dark brown. Sprinkle with flour and let them rise. Pour on the boiling water, spice with salt and lovage and bring to the boil over a moderate heat. Beat up the HONEY with some potato flour* and pour over the vegetable. Let it ferment for a short time.

* See Appendix.

HORS D'OEUVRES

CHAPTER V

HORS D'OEUVRES

American Sandwich Filling

Avocado Pear
Lemon Juice
Shrimps
Honey
Lettuce Leaves

Bananas
Cooked Chicken
Pineapple slices
Sea Salt, Cayenne Pepper

Prepare a smooth filling from the pulp of an avocado pear, crushed bananas, lemon juice, pieces of cooked chicken, shrimps, pineapple slices and HONEY to taste. Lightly sprinkle with sea salt and cayenne pepper and spread between slices of bread. Serve cold on lettuce leaves.

'Honolulu' Cheese Toast

4 slices White Bread and
  Butter
4 Pineapple rounds
2 teaspoonsful Honey

4 slices Ham
4 slices Cheese
Egg White
Red Currants for garnish

Grill the bread and butter. Cover with a slice of ham and pineapple. Drop half a teaspoon of HONEY on to each round of pineapple. To finish place a slice of cheese on each slice of bread on which there is a layer of beaten egg white. Grill until they are golden brown, and before serving garnish with red currants.

Spanish Rarebits

1 Onion	2-3 diced Tomatoes
1 finely chopped raw Pepper shell	7 oz. grated Emmental Cheese
2 Egg Yolks	½ teaspoonful Honey
Pinch Cayenne Pepper and Salt	Sherry Toast

Dice the onion and heat in butter, add the tomatoes and pepper shell. Steam until the liquid has evaporated. Mix in the cheese and remove from the heat. Mix the beaten egg yolks with HONEY, pepper and salt and a few drops of sherry and add to the mixture. Spread on fingers of toast. Drip on melted butter and grill. Serve hot.

Housewives' Honey Slices

Wholemeal Bread and Butter	Honey
Grated Almonds	Candied Fruit
	Apples and Grapes

Butter slices of wholemeal bread and spread with honey, grated almonds and finely cut candied fruit. Add thin slices of apple and decorate with grapes.

'Alhambra' Ham and Honey Toast

1 slice White Toast	1 slice cooked Ham
1 sliced Banana	1 ring tinned Pineapple
1 slice Cheese	Honey

Butter the slice of toast and spread with the slice of ham, banana, pineapple with a dab of honey in the middle and finish with the slice of cheese. Grill until the cheese melts.

44

'Hortense' Banana Rusk

4 Bananas
1 teaspoonful Lemon Juice
4 tablespoonsful chopped Walnuts
1 tablespoonful Honey
Pinch Chili Sauce
Rusks
Cherry Brandy

Crush the peeled bananas and mix with the HONEY and lemon juice. Add a pinch of chili sauce and the roughly chopped walnuts. Heap on to the rusks and spread with banana slices. In addition you can pour cherry brandy on to the rusks.

Honey Butter

1 cupful fresh Butter
1 teaspoonful Lemon Juice
6 teaspoonsful Honey
Ginger

Mix the butter with the HONEY and add the lemon juice and a pinch of ginger. This is excellent for a filling or for spreading on bread.

FISH

CHAPTER VI

FISH

Pike a l'Anglaise

1 lb. 2 oz. Pike	1 medium-sized Onion
9 oz. Tomato	Salt and Pepper
1 coffeespoonful Honey	1 glass Cider
Parsley or Watercress	

After well washing cut the pike into sections. Fry a medium-sized onion in fat and add the tomato seasoned with salt and pepper. Then add the HONEY and cider and pour the whole over the divided fish. Cook in a heated oven in a fire-proof dish. Garnish with parsley or watercress.

Trouts Cooked in a Paper Covering

Marinade:

4-5 Onions	4-5 Mushrooms
1-2 teaspoonsful Honey	1 glass White Wine
1-2 tablespoonsful Olive Oil	Caraway Seeds
Chopped Parsley	Salt, Chili Sauce

Place fairly small trout in the following marinade: Onions, mushrooms, HONEY, white wine, olive oil, caraway seeds, chopped parsley, salt and a trace of chili sauce. Then cover each individual trout with greaseproof paper and gently cook next to each other in a casserole dish. Serve with a butter sauce.

Steamed Sea Eel with Prunes

2 fresh sea Eels
Sliced Onions
6 large stoned Prunes
1 tablespoonful Honey
Olive Oil
2 glasses Red Wine
Lemon Peel, Salt, Pepper

Remove the skin from the eels. Cut into finger length strips, season and fry on both sides in hot olive oil. Surround with sliced onions and gently cook. Add a little water, half a lemon peel, and the red wine. The day before place the prunes in red wine to soak overnight, and then add to the sauce. Flavour with salt, pepper, and HONEY. Serve the pieces of eel hot in the sauce.

Estonian Fish in Gooseberry Sauce

1 lb. 2 oz. Haddock (Red Perch)
2 hard-boiled Eggs
2 tablespoonsful Butter
2 tablespoonsful Honey
$1\frac{1}{2}$ oz. Parsley Butter
$4\frac{1}{2}$ oz. Gooseberries
$1\frac{1}{2}$ oz. Flour
$\frac{1}{8}$ pint Cream
Salt
Lemon Juice

Cut up the haddock, wash, dry, sprinkle with lemon juice and leave to stand for thirty minutes. Place knobs of butter and seasoning in a casserole, add the pieces of fish and steam over a gentle heat. Quickly boil the green gooseberries, dry, and finely chop up with the hard-boiled eggs. Mix the flour with the butter, add the juice from the fish, the cream, and if necessary some milk, to make a creamy consistency. Beat up the gooseberries, and add some to the fish. Then beat in the HONEY, a pinch of salt, finely chopped parsley which has been mixed with the butter, and serve the fish in this sauce.

Scandinavian Pickled Fish

Fish according to quantity required
2 teaspoonsful Honey
Chopped Parsley and Onions
½ pint Rhine Wine
Salt, Pepper, Bay Leaf
2 Egg Yolks
½ cupful Sour Cream

Remove the bones and skin from pieces of fish and place them in the following pickle: Mix the wine with HONEY, salt, pepper, a bay leaf, onions and chopped parsley to taste, and let the fish soak in this mixture for one day. Then place in a greased dish, add the pickle having passed it through a sieve. Beat up a part of the pickle with the egg yolks and sour cream and add to the fish. Cook for about thirty-five minutes.

'Hongkong' Fish

1 Haddock
1 chopped Onion
Diced Carrots
1 Turnip
1 teaspoonful Honey
4 tablespoonsful Soya Sauce
Batter: 3 tablespoonsful Flour
2 tablespoonsful Water

2 tablespoonsful Oil
1 tablespoonful Wine Vinegar
Potato Flour*

Clean the fish, removing head and tail. Prepare a batter from the flour and water and turn the fish well in it. Then fry quickly in hot fat and remove from the pan. Add to the hot fat the chopped onion, diced carrots, turnips and fry. Later add the oil, HONEY, wine vinegar, soya sauce and a touch of potato flour.* Serve the fish hot in this sauce.

* See Appendix.

Indian Cinnamon Fish

1 lb. 10 oz. Red Perch	1½ oz. Flour
1 large Onion	6 large Tomatoes
2 sticks Cinnamon	1 teaspoonful Honey
3-4 tablespoonsful Oil	2-3 tablespoonsful Vinegar
Grated Cheese, Paprika, knobs of Butter, Salt and Pepper	1½ oz. Butter
	2 Egg Yolks

Cut the prepared fillets into small pieces and season. Skin and cut up the tomatoes and heat with the chopped onion, HONEY, spices, oil and vinegar. Take out the cinnamon, add the fish fillets and steam. Remove the fish from the sauce. Thicken with the flour and add the stock. Place the fish in a greased fire-proof dish, cover with the sauce, sprinkle with cheese and dot with knobs of butter. Grill until brown.

Icelandic White Herring

3 large white Herrings	3 medium-sized Onions
15 Pepper-corns	10 Pimentos
Spiced Cucumber	Sliced Lemons
Capers, Bay Leaf, Mustard	1 pint Sour Cream
1 tablespoonful Wine Vinegar	1 tablespoonful Honey

Clean, wash and bone the herrings and cut into pieces. Slice the onions and arrange in layers round the herrings. Beat up the pepper corns, pimentoes, roughly chopped spiced cucumber, mustard, sliced lemons, a few capers, one bay leaf, and just under the pint of sour cream, with the wine vinegar and HONEY. Pour this mixture over the herrings and let it stand for two days.

MEAT, GAME AND POULTRY

CHAPTER VII

MEAT

Rolled Meat Balls with Sage

Veal Cutlets	Slices of Ham
Slices of Cheese	1 Sage Leaf (per cutlet)
3 chopped Tomatoes	3 tablespoonsful Red Wine
½ tablespoonful Mustard	½ tablespoonful Honey
1 tablespoonful Flour	1 cupful Cream

Well pound thin veal cutlets, cover with a slice of raw ham, a slice of cheese and one sage leaf, roll up and fix with skewers. Fry the rolls in hot fat. Then add the tomatoes and red wine. Beat up some hot water with mustard and HONEY and pour over the meat, then cook until well done. Whip up the flour with the cream and thicken the sauce with this mixture, and serve hot.

Ham Rice with Bananas

9 oz. Rice	7 oz. Ham
2 oz. Butter	4 Bananas
Lemon Juice	1½ oz. melted Butter
Liquid Honey	

Wash the rice and cook in salt water, then dry. Cut up the ham into strips and heat in the butter. Add the rice and mix well. Halve the bananas, sprinkle with lemon juice and fry in melted butter until light brown. Pour on liquid HONEY to taste.

Tongue in Honey Sauce

1 fresh Tongue
1 coffeespoonful Sugar
Wine Vinegar
2 tablespoonsful Honey

3 tablespoonsful Butter
3 tablespoonsful Flour
Raisins

Gently cook the tongue, drain and cut into slices. Fry the butter and sugar until golden-brown. Add the flour and fill up with tongue stock. Add wine vinegar to taste. Cook a handful of raisins and HONEY with the meat, and serve the tongue in this mixture.

Asiatic Honey Ham

1 lb. 2 oz. Ham
1 cupful Sherry
Chili Sauce

1 cupful Honey
Potato Flour*

Place the ham in a pan and add a mixture of HONEY and sherry. Steam the ham over a gentle heat, turn frequently and cover with the liquid. When the ham is tender, remove it from the pan and cut into small pieces. Thicken the sauce with potato flour, and flavour with a few drops of chili sauce.

Pork Cutlets

Pork Cutlets
2 teaspoonsful Honey

3 tablespoonsful Red
 Cranberry Jelly
4 ground Cloves

Quickly fry pork cutlets in hot fat, season and cover with a mixture of cranberry jelly, HONEY, and cloves. Then cook for about fifteen minutes in a moderate oven.

* See Appendix.

Sweet and Sour Pork

1 lb. 2 oz. Rib, Neck, or Cutlets Pork	1 tablespoonful Vinegar
1 tablespoonful Sherry	½ tablespoonful Soya Sauce

Batter:

5 tablespoonsful Flour	5 tablespoonsful Water
1 teaspoonful Soda	1 Egg White

1 Green Pepper	3 tablespoonsful Vinegar
1 Red Pepper	2 tablespoonsful Honey
2 tablespoonsful Soya Sauce	Cornflour

Cut up the pork into small pieces and cover with the mixture of sherry, vinegar and soya sauce. Leave to stand for thirty minutes. Prepare a thin batter from the flour, soda, water and egg white, and turn the pieces of meat in the batter and fry in melted lard until brown. Then remove. Cut up the husks of the peppers into small pieces and quickly fry. Add the soya sauce, vinegar, HONEY and thicken with cornflour to form a sauce. Add the fried meat to the sauce and toss for a short time.

Beef with Honey-Cherry Glacé

Sugar	Butter
¼ pint Gravy	Cherry juice
1 tablespoonful Honey	

Gently cook a thin joint of beef. Fry a few spoonfuls of sugar in hot butter. Add the meat to the pan and brown on all sides. Add the gravy. Whip up several tablespoonsful of cherry juice with the HONEY and add to the gravy. Cover the meat well with the juice.

Hawaiian Calf's Sweetbread

7 oz. Sweetbreads
1 teaspoonful chopped Parsley
2 teaspoonsful Capers
2 tablespoonsful Sweet Cream
½ teaspoonful Honey
Salt and Red Pepper

2 teaspoonsful chopped Onion
2 tablespoonsful White Wine
1 Banana
1 Egg Yolk
1 tablespoonful Breadcrumbs
Pineapple

Soak the washed sweetbreads in gently boiling water, remove the skin and dice. Cook the chopped onion and parsley in butter. Add the sweetbreads for a short time together with the white wine, capers and the finely chopped banana. Whip up egg milk from the sweet cream, egg yolk, HONEY, breadcrumbs, and a pinch of salt and red pepper. Mix with the sweetbreads and place on a greased fire-proof dish. Cover with slices of pineapple and knobs of butter and cook in the oven for thirty minutes.

Fine Lamb Cutlets

Lamb Cutlets
Milk
Breadcrumbs
Water Melon

Beaten Egg
Honey
Sea Salt, Cayenne Pepper
Grapes

Turn the cutlets in a mixture of beaten egg, milk, and HONEY. Cover with breadcrumbs and fry in hot fat. Sprinkle sea salt and cayenne pepper on to the cutlets and top with a slice of water melon and some grapes.

58

Fine Pork Rolls on Jelly

Pork according to
requirements
Honey
Onions
6 leaves Gelatine

Lemon Peel
Oil
Salt, Pepper, Bay Leaf
1 pint Stock

Cut the crackling of the pork into hand-sized pieces. Cover with a thin slice of pork, season and spread on the pork a mixture of grated lemon peel and a little HONEY. Then firmly roll together and fasten with string. Cover the rolls with a mixture of two-thirds water and one-third oil, onions, salt, pepper, one bay leaf, and cook until the crackling is soft. Place on a dish which has been rinsed in cold water, and cover with the gravy made after sieving the pint of stock with gelatine.

'Copenhagen' Lamb

2 lb. Lamb
1 teaspoonful Flour
3 Egg Yolks
1 tablespoonful Honey
9 oz. Crab

1 Onion
Salt
1 tablespoonful Lemon
Juice
Salt, Black Pepper
Handful young Peas

Dice the lamb. Heat the onion in butter and add the meat, pinch of salt and flour. Cook until the onion is bright yellow and then fill up with water. Hardly cook the meat. Make a sauce from the meat juice beaten up with the egg yolks, lemon juice, HONEY, salt and black pepper, crab and peas. Add the meat to this mixture and let it soak well in the juice.

59

Yen Lies Roast Pork

2 lb. Shoulder of Pork
Sweet and Sour Pears

Sauce:
3 cups Chicken Broth
4 teaspoonsful Honey
4 teaspoonsful Sugar
3 teaspoonsful Soya Sauce
1 teaspoonful Salt

Cut the pork into four pieces. Place in the sauce made from mixing the above ingredients, and leave to stand for two hours. Turn frequently in the sauce. Then roast in a medium hot oven with part of the sauce. Serve with sweet and sour pears.

Hortobagyi-kapuszta

Bacon
Chopped Pork
Chopped Onions
Beef Stock
Sour Cream

Sauerkraut
Salt, Pepper, Garlic
Green Pepper
Chopped Dill
1 tablespoonful Honey

Cover a deep casserole with thin slices of bacon and layer about one inch of thick raw sauerkraut on top of the bacon. Then add the same amount of chopped pork which has been seasoned with salt, pepper and a touch of garlic, and a layer of chopped onions with strips of green pepper. End with a layer of raw sauerkraut. Cover the whole with beef stock and cook for thirty minutes in a medium-hot oven. Then sprinkle with finely chopped dill. Pour on sour cream which has been whipped with the HONEY. Heat once again until really tender.

CHAPTER VIII

GAME AND POULTRY

Glazed Game Steaks

4 Steaks	1 cupful Brown Sugar
½ cupful Honey	½ cupful Orange Juice
Sea Salt, Cayenne Pepper	Pineapple

Place the steaks of any game according to taste under the grill and cover with a mixture of sugar, HONEY, and orange juice until this is glazed on the steaks. Finally carefully sprinkle with sea salt and cayenne pepper. Serve with pineapple slices.

Chinese Duck

4 teaspoonsful Honey	4 teaspoonsful Sugar
1 teaspoonful Salt	1 teaspoonful Soya Sauce
1 cupful Chicken Broth or Stock	1 Duck
	Pineapple

Beat up the HONEY, sugar, salt, soya sauce, and stock. Place the duck in this sauce and allow to stand for two hours. Place some of the sauce in a casserole and roast the duck in a medium-hot oven for two hours until it is golden brown. Fill up with pineapple juice, thicken with potato flour* and surround with pineapple slices.

* See Appendix.

61

Fillet of Venison in Honey-Cream Sauce

Venison
¼ pint Cream
2-3 tablespoonsful Flour
1 tablespoonful Sugar
1 tablespoonful Honey
Lemon Peel and Salt

Pickle:
Vinegar
Bay Leaf, Spices, Cloves
Onion, Salt

Skin a fillet of venison, season with salt and pepper, pickle, thickly cover with fat and then fry. Use some of the pickle, which consists of vinegar, a bay leaf, spices, cloves, an onion and a pinch of salt, for cooking the meat. When the fillet is tender, add the cream which has been beaten with the flour. Fry the sugar in fat until brown and then mix with chopped lemon peel, HONEY, and a pinch of salt. Add to the sauce. Bring to the boil, strain through a sieve and serve.

Duaz-Fenjo

1 Goose
Salt, Honey, Cloves
Castor Sugar
Grated Almonds
Tin of Cherries

Stuffing:
Chopped Apples, Prunes
Breadcrumbs
1 small glass Brandy
3 tablespoonsful Honey

Salt the inside of the goose and smear the outside with HONEY. Garnish with cloves. Stuff the goose with a mixture of apples, prunes, breadcrumbs, brandy and HONEY. Sew up well and roast in a hot oven until the outside is crisp and brown. Sprinkle with castor sugar and surround with grated almonds and tinned cherries.

Mexican Chicken

1 Chicken	Juniper Berries
2 tablespoonful Honey	Potato Flour*
Bacon	Cream
Vine Leaves	

Pickle:

1 pint Water	1 small Leek
¾ pint Vinegar	15 Cloves, 15 Peppercorns,
1 pint sour Red Currant Juice	5 Pimentos, 10 Juniper Berries
Peel of 1 Lemon	2 Bay Leaves, 1 stalk Rosemary
1 teaspoonful chopped Onion	1 stalk Thyme

Wash and clean the chicken, and cover with the boiling hot pickle, which consists of just under the pint of water, vinegar, red currant juice, peel of a lemon, chopped onions, leek, cloves, peppercorns, pimentos, juniper berries, bay leaves, rosemary and thyme mixed well together and brought to the boil. After this has cooled add the HONEY to the pickle, and leave the chicken to stand for five days completely covered by this pickle. Remove and cover with slices of bacon, stuff with vine leaves and juniper berries and roast in butter. Fill a pan with the sauce and heat the chicken in it, and thicken the sauce with potato flour* and cream.

* See Appendix.

Duck with Orange Sauce

1 Duck	Meat Stock
1 oz. Sugar	Potato Flour
1 tablespoonful Wine Vinegar	1 tablespoonful Honey
	Half a Lemon
2 Oranges	

Take the duck and roast for a good twenty-five minutes in a hot oven. Remove the breast and cut into thin slices. Cook up the remainder of the duck with meat stock and thicken with potato flour.*
Brown the sugar in a pan and dissolve in the wine vinegar. Beat up in the liquid the HONEY, and add the juice of the oranges and half a lemon and a spoonful of finely chopped orange peel. Bring the ingredients to the boil in the sauce and then pour over the breast of the duck.

* See Appendix.

STEWED FRUITS, COLD DISHES AND DRINKS

CHAPTER IX

STEWED FRUIT

Karlsbad Apple Puree

2¾ lb. cooking Apples	¼ pint light White Wine
Cinnamon	3 Cloves
4 tablespoonsful Sugar	Lemon Peel
Cornflour	2 tablespoonsful Honey
Soaked Raisins	

Wash the apples, dry and quarter, finely chop, the peel included. Cook gently in the wine with the cinnamon, cloves, sugar and a piece of lemon peel. Thicken with cornflour and shortly before serving add the HONEY. Cover with soaked raisins.

'Beauharnais' Stewed Plums

Dried Plums	Cinnamon, Orange Peel
Water, Red Wine	1 tablespoonful Honey
1 small glass Vanilla	
Liqueur	

Cook the dried plums with sugar, cinnamon, orange peel, water and red wine. Then remove the stones and replace them with blanched almonds. Layer the plums in a glass dish. Beat up the juice with the HONEY and vanilla liqueur, and pour the mixture over the plums. Serve with wafer biscuits.

Preserves Using Honey

1 lb. Fruit   ½ lb. pure Honey

The hard fruits like apples and pears are most
suitable, but also plums, peaches, apricots and
quinces can be preserved in HONEY. Use in the
proportions given above. Carefully select the
fruit, clean, halve and firmly pack into a well
sterilised glass · jar or pot. Then the HONEY is
cooked, skimmed and poured hot over the fruit.
Seal the pot with greaseproof paper to preserve the
fruit. Ensure that the honey is one and a half
inches thick above the fruit so that, in crystallising,
the quantity does not decrease. The fruit and
honey can also be cooked together for a short time.

Honey Fruit Dish

¼ pint Grape Juice   1 tablespoonful Honey
1 Apple   1 Orange
1 Banana   1 tablespoonful Sweet
8 Hazel Nuts grated   Cream

Mix the juice, and HONEY with the cream. Soak the
peeled and sliced apple, sliced orange, banana, in
this mixture and sprinkle with nuts. This dish can
also be made from plums, peaches, grapes,
apricots, strawberries, raspberries, melons or pineapple.

CHAPTER X

COLD DISHES AND DRINKS

'Aurora' Fruit Dish

3 tablespoonsful Sago
1 pint Fruit Juice or White
   Wine
Cinnamon and Cloves

1¾ pints Water
4 tablespoonsful Honey
Macaroons

Cook the sago in the water until it thickens. Add the fruit juice or white wine, and spice with cinnamon and cloves. After cooling add the HONEY, and decorate with tiny macaroons.

Fruit and Honey Milk

10 Hazel Nuts grated
Juice of half a Lemon

3 tablespoonsful Honey
1 glass Buttermilk

Beat up the grated nuts, HONEY and lemon juice with the glass of buttermilk until it foams. Serve cold.

Honey-Orange Cocktail

3 tablespoonsful Honey   ½ pint Orange Juice
Sea Salt

Mix the HONEY with the orange juice, adding a pinch of sea salt. Serve on crushed ice in cocktail glasses.

Apricot Cold Dish

4½ oz. fresh Apricots   Sugar
2 tablespoonsful Honey   ¼ pint Grape Juice
1 cupful Water   Macaroons

Slice the fresh apricots and sprinkle with a little sugar. Beat up the HONEY with the grape juice and water and pour over the apricots. Let them stand for one hour, and serve with macaroons.

Honey Lemonade

1 lb. 2 oz. Honey   3½ oz. Lemon Juice
Mineral Water

Mix the HONEY with the pure lemon juice. For every 1-1½ ounces add one small bottle of mineral water. Whisk the drink until the contents are well blended. Honey lemonade is a very refreshing drink on hot days, but it is also very popular and digestible as a night-cap.

Buttermilk Dessert

1¾ pints cold Buttermilk
5 slices grated Pumper-
  nickel Bread*
4 tablespoonsful Honey

1 Lemon
2½ oz. Raisins
3 tablespoonsful Vanilla
  Sugar

Mix well together the cold buttermilk, juice and grated rind of half a lemon, the grated Pumpernickel bread,* raisins, HONEY, and vanilla sugar, and serve cold.

Honey Coffee

1 glass hot full cream Milk
1 tablespoonful Honey

1 teaspoonful ground Coffee

Mix together the hot milk, coffee, and HONEY. Cold milk can also be used.

Milk and Honey Mix

1 pint Milk
Raspberry Juice

3 teaspoonsful Honey
Soda Water

Whisk up the milk and HONEY until it foams. Add a little raspberry juice, and half fill the glasses with this mixture. Fill them up with soda water.

Chinatown Juice

1 Lemon
3 tablespoonsful Honey

1 cupful ice-cold Water

Mix the juice of the lemon with the ice-cold water and HONEY.

* See Appendix.

71

'Manhattan' Honey Drink

1 cupful ice-cold Milk
2 teaspoonsful Honey

4 tablespoonsful Tomato
Juice
1 teaspoonful Lemon Juice

Beat the milk with tomato juice. Add the HONEY and lemon juice.

'Lukullus' Honey Drink

9 oz. Curds
½ pint Milk
Sugar

4 tablespoonsful Honey
¼ pint Fruit Juice
Pinch of Ginger and Cocoa

Beat up the curds with the HONEY, milk, fruit juice and sugar to taste. Sprinkle with a pinch of ginger and cocoa, and serve cold.

Honey Ice Shake

1 glass Milk
1 tablespoonful Honey

1 Egg Yolk

Beat up the milk with the egg yolk and HONEY, and serve hot or cold.

'Ceylon' or 'Indian' Honey Tea

4 teaspoonsful Tea
5 cupfuls Soda Water
5 tablespoonsful Orange
   Juice
2 cupfuls hot Water

1 teaspoonful Cloves
½ cupful Honey
3 tablespoonsful Lemon
   Juice

Mix the tea with the cloves and add the soda water. Leave to stand for five minutes. Sieve and add the HONEY. Then add the orange juice and lemon juice, and finally pour the hot water over the mixture.

Health Cocktail

Rhubarb Juice
2 tablespoonsful Honey

3½ oz. Strawberries

Mix freshly crushed rhubarb juice with the crushed strawberries and HONEY. Serve cold.

CAKES AND PASTRIES

CHAPTER XI

CAKES AND PASTRIES

Honey Paste with Puff Pastry

5 oz. Flour	1 teaspoonful Baking
5 oz. Dried Curds	Powder
1 teaspoonful Salt	5 oz. Margarine or Butter
	Almonds and Cherries

Make the puff pastry by sifting the flour, baking powder together. Add the dried curds, margarine and salt, and knead well together. Roll out, work well together and once more roll out. Cool the dough before the kneading. Thinly roll out the curd puff pastry, spread with HONEY and fill with peeled almonds and candied cherries. Make into finger-thick rolls and cook in a hot oven.

Moorish Kisses

Biscuits or Macaroons	Milk
Beaten Egg	Honey
Chopped Almonds	Glacé Cherries
Pistachio Nuts	

Soak small round biscuits or macaroons in milk and turn in beaten egg. Cook on both sides in hot fat until golden brown. Spread with a paste of warmed HONEY and finely chopped almonds. Top with a glacé cherry or a pistachio nut.

Basle Honey Cakes

2 lb. Honey
1 lb. 2 oz. chopped Almonds
1½-2 oz. Cinnamon
1 Lemon and 1 Orange Peel
1 oz. Potassium Carbonate
2½ lb. sifted Flour

1 lb. 2 oz. Sugar
3½ oz. Candied Peel
2 teaspoonsful Clove Powder
1 teaspoonful Mace
Cherry Brandy: 1 Liqueur glass

Boil the HONEY and add the sugar. Remove the saucepan from the heat and continue to beat until everything is cooled to hand temperature. Then, still beating the mixture, add the spices, the almonds, chopped candied peel, cinnamon, clove powder, finely chopped peel of the lemon and orange, mace, potassium carbonate which has been dissolved in a little of the cherry brandy, the remainder of the liqueur glass of cherry brandy, and finally the flour. Firmly knead the dough and place it in a warm spot for twenty-four hours. Later knead it once again, roll it out until ⅛ in. thick and cut into card-sized rectangles. Then place next to each other on a well-greased and floured baking tray and cook in in a medium-hot oven for twenty to twenty-five minutes. While still hot, cut the rectangles through once, and spread with icing when cool and separate.

Vienna Slices

2½ oz. Honey
2 oz. chopped Almonds
3 Cloves
9 oz. Flour
1 Egg Yolk

2 Rolls
1 coffeespoonful Cinnamon
Grated Peel of an Orange or
Lemon
9 oz. Sugar
½ pint Cream

Warm the HONEY and add the finely grated breadcrumbs from the two rolls, the chopped almonds, cinnamon, cloves, also finely chopped, and the grated peel of the lemon or orange. Form a thick dough from these ingredients and cook. After cooling make hazel-nut sized balls. Make a pastry from the flour, sugar, egg yolk, and cream. Then roll out until about $\frac{1}{16}$ in. thick, cover half the pastry with the balls spread with beaten egg and firmly place the other half on top. Cut in slices and cook on a greased baking tray.

Nougat Pyramids

3½ oz. Honey
9 oz. Flour
½ grated Lemon Peel
2 tablespoonsful Arrak
5 oz. Sugar

Cinnamon, crushed Clove,
Mace
2 oz. Nougat
Pinch Ammonium
Carbonate

Melt the HONEY and sugar and blend well by placing them in a basin within a bowl of hot water. When almost cool, mix with the flour, spices, lemon peel and grated nougat. Finally stir in the ammonium carbonate which has been dissolved in the arrak. Roll out the pastry until $\frac{1}{4}$ in. thick, cut into triangles, place on a greased baking tray and cook in a moderate oven.

Prague Nut Roll

1 lb. 2 oz. Flour
2 tablespoonsful Sugar
2 Egg Yolks
Warm Milk
¾ oz. Yeast
2 oz. Butter
Pinch of Salt

Nut Filling:
¼ pint Milk
2 teaspoonsful Rum
Pinch of Cinnamon
12 oz. grated Walnuts
10 tablespoonsful Honey
3 Cloves
Grated Lemon Peel

Prepare a dough from the flour, yeast, sugar, butter, egg yolks and salt. Later add a little warm milk. Then roll out thinly and cover with a nut filling. To make this filling mix the walnuts, milk, HONEY, rum, cloves, a pinch of cinnamon and grated lemon peel. Roll up the pastry and cook until golden brown. Sprinkle with castor sugar.

Florentine Quince Tart

1 lb. 2 oz. Quinces
3 tablespoonsful Sugar
9 oz. Flour
4½ oz. Butter
Vanilla essence

3 Eggs
2 tablespoonsful Honey
Pinch of Salt
1 Egg

Boil the quinces, remove the juice and pass through a hair sieve. Make a thick juice from the whites of three eggs, sugar and HONEY, and stir into the quinces. Make a short pastry from the flour, salt, butter and one egg. Fit and trim on to a dish and cook until light brown. Cover with the quince mixture and top with stiffly beaten egg whites. Season with sugar and vanilla essence and cook until the egg whites begin to brown.

'Sassnitz' Honey Tart

7 oz. Flour
3 oz. Honey
Icing Sugar

Pistachio Nuts
Candied Fruits
5 oz. Butter

Filling:
1 cupful Raisins
1 cupful chopped Lemon or Orange Peel
1 tablespoonful Brown Sugar
2 tablespoonsful Milk
2 tablespoonsful melted Butter
1 coffeespoonful Cinnamon

Beat up the flour with the butter and HONEY. Halve the dough and cover one half with the following mixture: Mix well together the raisins, lemon or orange peel, brown sugar, milk, melted butter and cinnamon. Cover with the remaining half of dough. Cook the tart for thirty minutes in a medium hot oven. Decorate with icing made from icing sugar, a little water and lemon juice, and top with pistachio nuts and candied fruits.

Honey Bee Cake

7 oz. Flour
Pinch of Salt
2 teaspoonsful Vinegar
½ oz. Yeast
Water

Filling:
4½ oz. ground Almonds
3 teaspoonsful Honey
7 oz. Castor Sugar
Vanilla flavouring

Knead a dough from the flour, yeast, salt, a little water, and the vinegar. Let it rise once and spread evenly with the following mixture: Almonds, HONEY, castor sugar and vanilla flavouring. Stir well before spreading on the dough and cook in a medium-hot oven until golden brown.

Cobble Slices

4½ oz. Honey
2 oz. Sugar
1 oz. diced Candied Peel
½ teaspoonful ground
  Cinnamon
1 tablespoonful Rum
2 oz. Cornflour
4½ oz. Icing Sugar
Lemon Peel grated

2 oz. Butter
1 oz. ground Almonds
1 Egg
Cloves, Ginger
7 oz. Flour
½ oz. Baking Powder
1 teaspoonful Raspberry
  Essence

Heat the HONEY with the butter and sugar. Beat up with the almonds, diced candied peel, egg and ground cinnamon. According to taste add ground cloves, a pinch of ginger and the rum. Mix the flour with the cornflour and baking powder, and knead together with the other ingredients. Shape the dough into a roll, cut into slices and cook for twenty minutes on a greased baking tray. Beat up the icing sugar with the raspberry essence and lemon peel, and then spread on the slices.

Straubing Honey Cake

1 lb. Almonds
¼ lb. Honey
6-8 tablespoonsful Water

¾ lb. Sugar
3½ oz. grated Chocolate
Egg White

Stir the almonds, sugar, HONEY, chocolate and water in a saucepan over a gentle heat until the mixture has blended and no longer sticks to the saucepan. After cooling, roll out the mixture until finger thick and cut out into attractive shapes. Then spread the cakes with egg white. Sugar can be sprinkled on top. Quickly cook in a moderate oven.

Honey Cake

10 oz. Flour
3 tablespoonsful Milk
3 oz. Butter
½ teaspoonful Salt
1-2 tablespoonsful Water
¾ oz. Yeast
1½ oz. Honey
1 Egg

From these ingredients make a dough, let it rise and then cook in a bread tin. After cooling, cut the cake into finger-thick slices, which can then be re-cooked until light brown, if desired.

Poppy Twists

1 lb. 2 oz. Flour
1 oz. Yeast
½ cupful tepid Milk
3 tablespoonsful Sour Cream
7 oz. Butter
1 tablespoonful Sugar
6 Eggs

Poppy filling:
9 oz. ground Poppy Seeds
2 Cloves
Grated peel of half a Lemon
1 pint hot Milk
5 oz. Honey
Cinnamon
Icing Sugar

Sieve the seasoned flour into a bowl and rub in the butter. Whisk the yeast with the sugar and tepid milk and pour on to the flour. Then add the eggs and sour cream. Knead this mixture into a smooth dough. Leave to rise in a warm place and roll out until ⅛ in. thick. Cut into squares and cover with the poppy filling. This is made from the hot milk beaten up with the ground poppy seeds, to which is added the HONEY, cloves, cinnamon and grated peel of half a lemon. Cook the mixture thoroughly and when cool spread on the squares. Roll up, dab with egg and cook in a hot oven. Dust with icing sugar.

Ginger and Honey Bread

2 lb. Honey	2 lb. Sugar
5 lb. Flour	9 oz. chopped Almonds
2 oz. chopped Bitter Almonds	Pinch of Cardamom,
	Pinch of grated Nutmeg
1 oz. Cinnamon	Pinch of Pepper
½ oz. Ginger	1 glass Rum

Boil the HONEY with the sugar. Stir together the flour, chopped almonds, bitter almonds, cardamom, cinnamon, grated nutmeg, ginger and pepper. Add the glass of rum, and finally add the cooled HONEY to the other ingredients and knead to a dough. Cook this bread in a baking tin for one hour.

Hamburg Honey Cakes

5 oz. Honey	3½ oz. Sugar
9 oz. Flour	½ small packet Gingerbread Spice
4½ oz. chopped Candied Peel	1½ oz. grated Chocolate
Pinch of Ammonium Carbonate and Potassium Bicarbonate	Cashew Nuts

Stir together with HONEY and sugar. Knead well together the flour, gingerbread spice, chopped candied peel, grated chocolate, and the pinch of ammonium carbonate and potassium bicarbonate. Make sure these ingredients have been well blended together before adding the HONEY and sugar. Roll out until finger thick and cut into rectangles. Spread with HONEY and top with a cashew nut. Leave to stand for a night and then cook in a moderate oven.

Banana Canapes

1 cupful Cream
2 heaped teaspoonsful Baking Powder
2 tablespoonsful Honey
2 Bananas

2 cupfuls Brown Flour
Pinch of Salt
1 Egg Yolk and White
Castor Sugar

Beat up the cream, flour, baking powder, salt and HONEY to a stiff consistency. Beat in the egg yolk and beaten egg white, and then add the sliced bananas to the mixture. Place in a pan of hot fat in spoonfuls. Sprinkle with castor sugar and serve immediately.

'Lugano' Apple Tart

9 oz. Flour
Pinch of Salt
2 tablespoonsful Cream
6½ oz. Butter
2 Egg Yolks

Filling:
3 oz. Butter
Orange Peel
⅓ pint White Wine
1 lb. 2 oz. sliced Apples
2½ oz. Sugar
1 teaspoonful Cinnamon
Honey

Make a short pastry from the flour, butter, pinch of salt, egg yolks and cream. Roll out and place on a tart dish. Half cook, and when cool, cover with the following filling: Steam the sliced apples, butter, sugar, a little orange peel, cinnamon, in the white wine. When cool, place on the pastry and richly coat with HONEY. With the remains of the pastry, arrange strips over the tart in a lattice design. After cooking at a medium temperature, spread with lemon glazing.

Christmas Tree Decorations

10 oz. Rye Flour*
2 Eggs
Pinch of Cinnamon
Handful grated Almonds

5 oz. Honey
10 Cloves
Pinch Sodium Bicarbonate
Finely chopped peel of 8-10 Oranges

Blend together the flour, HONEY, eggs, cloves, cinnamon, sodium bicarbonate, grated almonds, and the orange peel. Roll out the pastry until $\frac{1}{4}$ in. thick and cut into circles, hearts, stars and angel shapes and other designs. In every figure pierce a small hole to enable a thread to be passed through when tying to the tree. Cook the figures quickly on a greased baking tray, spread with egg white, and decorate with coloured sugar grains. As an alternative, the figures can be covered with an icing, made from icing sugar, water and lemon juice.

Nürnberg Pastries

5 oz. Honey
1½ oz. halved Almonds
1 oz. chopped Candied Peel
5 oz. Flour

2 Eggs
1 oz. grated Orange Peel
Crushed Cloves, Cinnamon

Beat up the HONEY with the eggs until well blended. Stir in the halved almonds, grated orange peel, chopped candied peel, crushed cloves, cinnamon, and the flour. Roll out the pastry very thinly and place on a well greased baking tray. Cook in a moderate oven. Cut the pastry into strips and return to the oven for a short time to dry before cooling.

* See Appendix.

Honey Curds Cake

Pastry
4½ oz. Honey
Pinch crushed Cinnamon

1 lb. 2 oz. Curds
4 Egg Yolks and Whites

Place the following filling between two layers of pastry: Beat well together the curds and HONEY, egg yolks and a pinch of crushed cinnamon. Finally stir in the beaten egg whites. Cook in a moderately hot oven for thirty minutes, and then sprinkle with cinnamon.

'Insterburg' Honey Gingerbread

9 oz. Honey
3 lb. 6 oz. Flour
12 oz. Candied Peel
2 Lemons
Mace and Baking Powder

9 oz. Sugar
¼ pint Cherry Brandy
1 lb. 2 oz. chopped Almonds
Clove and Vanilla Essence
Almonds and Candied
    Ginger

Heat the HONEY and sugar until well blended together. Add the flour, cherry brandy, finely chopped candied peel, chopped almonds, the peel of the two lemons, a little clove and vanilla essence, mace and baking powder. Knead the dough firmly, roll out, cook and while still warm cut into rectangles. Decorate with almonds and candied ginger.

Vanilla Gingerbread

1 pint Honey
1 lb. 2 oz. Flour
9 oz. Castor Sugar
Peeled rind of 1 Lemon
1 tablespoonful hot Water
Few drops of Rum

1 liqueur glass Vanilla
  Liqueur
1½ teaspoonsful Baking
  Powder
¼ dessertspoonful
  Cinnamon
3 tablespoonsful Icing Sugar

Warm just under the pint of HONEY with the liqueur glass of vanilla liqueur. To the flour, add the baking powder, castor sugar, cinnamon and the peeled rind of the lemon. Mix the ingredients together and then stir in the HONEY. Place on a floured board, cut into the shapes desired and cook in a moderate oven. When cool, cover with white rum and sugar glazing made by mixing the icing sugar with the hot water and a few drops of rum.

Indio Cake

5 oz. Flour
5 oz. Sugar
Honey

5 oz. Butter
Lemon Juice

Brown the flour and butter in a frying pan. Sprinkle the sugar with lemon juice until it is damp. Pour the sugar on to a greased surface and add the flour and butter mixture. Knead with greased hands and roll out the pastry until paper thin. Divide the dough several times and finally shape into finger-thick rolls. Place these next to each other on a greased baking tray and cook in a moderate oven until brown. Eat warm sprinkled with HONEY.

Honey-Nut Croissant

7 oz. Flour
Pinch of Salt

½ oz. Yeast
2 tablespoonsful Vinegar

Nut filling:
2 tablespoonsful Sugar
2 tablespoonsful Honey
2 oz. fine Biscuit crumbs

5 oz. grated Hazel and
    Walnuts
Milk

Prepare a dough from the flour, yeast, pinch of salt and vinegar. Roll out thinly and spread with the following nut filling: Heat the grated hazel and walnuts, sugar, fine biscuit crumbs, HONEY and a little milk but do not overcook. After cooling the mixture should be smooth. According to taste a small or a large croissant can be made. Spread with beaten egg and cook in a moderate oven.

Special Fruit Slices

10 oz. Flour
3 tablespoonsful Honey
Pinch of Cinnamon
1 coffeespoonful Sodium
    Bicarbonate

6 oz. Sugar
2 Eggs
Crushed Cloves
Figs, chopped Nuts,
    Raisins, Almonds

Knead well together the flour, sugar, HONEY, eggs, cinnamon, cloves and sodium bicarbonate. Halve the mixture and roll out each section until ½ in. thick. Cover one half with finely chopped figs, chopped nuts and raisins. Place the other half firmly on top. Cook in a moderate oven on a greased baking tray. After cooling, cut into quarters and cover with sugar glazing or almonds.

Honey Cake with Sour Cream

3½ oz. Sugar
¼ pint sour Cream
½ teaspoonful Baking
    Powder

3 tablespoonsful Honey
4 oz. Flour
Handful of Raisins

Beat the sugar and the cream and then add the flour mixed with the baking powder, the raisins and HONEY. Place the mixture in a greased baking tin and cook for thirty-five minutes. This can be eaten for breakfast spread with butter.

Honey Fruit Cake

2 tablespoonsful Potato
    Flour*
¾ cupful Honey
1½ cupfuls Currants
2 tablespoonsful Butter
4 tablespoonsful Lemon
    Juice

Water
1½ cupfuls Raisins
1½ cupfuls Sultanas
1 tablespoonful chopped
    Orange Peel
Pinch of Salt

Mix the flour with a little cold water to form a dough. Add the HONEY, raisins, currants, sultanas, butter, a half cupful of water, chopped orange peel, lemon juice and a pinch of salt. Stir in a saucepan for three to four minutes until it thickens. Wrap in puff pastry, and place in a baking tin and cook in a hot oven for thirty minutes.

* See Appendix.

Gourmet's Tart

½ lb. Sugar
9 oz. ground Almonds
2 Lemons
5 Walnuts
Castor Sugar

⅓ pint Water
1 oz. Apricot Jam
1 oz. chopped Candied Peel
¼ lb. Honey
Fruit Jellies and Candied
Orange Peel

Brown the sugar and water in a frying pan. Add the sweet ground almonds, an ounce of apricot jam, taking care to extract any fruit, the grated peel of the two lemons, the chopped candied peel and the walnuts finely grated. Stir this over a low heat until it thickens. Add the HONEY. Spread on a baking tray that has been covered with rice paper. A very low oven temperature is required as this tart must not cook—only dry. Sprinkle with castor sugar and decorate with fruit jellies and candied orange peel.

SWEET DISHES AND SWEETS

CHAPTER XII

SWEET DISHES

Honey Dip with Fruit

Cream Cheese portions
1 tablespoonful Honey
Bananas, Oranges, Figs,
    Dates and Raisins

½ tin condensed Milk
1 tablespoonful Wheat Germ

Gently heat a portion of cream cheese. When soft mix with the condensed milk, HONEY and wheat germ. Place the following on top of the dip—crushed bananas, chopped oranges, figs, dates and a handful of raisins.

Pastor Kneipp's Raw Food Dish

9 oz. Curds
2 grated Apples
1 tablespoonful Lemon
    Juice
2 teaspoonsful Oats

4 tablespoonsful Honey
¼ pint Milk
1 teaspoonful chopped Nuts
1 teaspoonful Linseed Seeds

Beat the above ingredients well together.

Turkish Kadayif

1 lb. 2 oz. Vermicelli	2 cupfuls Water
1 pint Water	14 oz. Sugar
5 oz. Honey	1 pint Sweet Cream
2 leaves White Gelatine	4 tablespoonsful Sugar
2 teaspoonsful Honey	

Layer the vermicelli finger-deep on a baking tray. Sprinkle with the two cupfuls of water and cook in a moderate oven. Make a sugar syrup from the pint of water, sugar and HONEY. Cook until blended and then pour over the browned noodles. Beat up stiffly just under the pint of cream, stir in the dissolved leaves of white gelatine, sugar and HONEY. Layer the whipped cream finger-thick on half of the noodles. When set and completely firm place the remaining noodles on top. When the tart has set, cut and decorate with candied fruits.

Turkish Peach Cream

3 tinned or fresh Peaches	2 Egg Whites
Cherry Brandy	1 pint Milk
3 Egg Yolks	Nuts or Cherries to decorate
6 tablespoonsful Honey	

Halve the peaches and place each in a champagne glass. Sprinkle with a few drops of cherry brandy. Beat together the egg yolks and the HONEY and add the egg whites, which have been stiffly beaten. Heat the milk and quickly beat into the mixture. Place the bowl in a bowl of hot water and continue to beat until the cream thickens. Do not cook. Pour the cooled cream over the peaches. Deck with almonds, pistachio nuts or cherries.

Zürich Honey Pudding

2 oz. firm Honey
2 tablespoonsful Sugar
2 Eggs
2 oz. Flour
1 tablespoonful Yellow
  Chartreuse

4 oz. Brown Breadcrumbs
Juice of half a Lemon
1 oz. melted Butter
2 tablespoonsful cold Milk
Whites of four Eggs

Beat well together the HONEY, breadcrumbs, sugar, lemon juice, eggs, melted butter, flour, milk, and yellow chartreuse. Add the four stiffly beaten egg whites. Fill a greased pudding bowl with this mixture and place in a bowl of boiling water. Then place in a hot oven for thirty minutes. Remove the pudding bowl from the bowl of hot water, leave to stand for one minute and then turn out. Cover the pudding with melted HONEY.

Vanilla Bananas

Halved Bananas
Honey
Lemon Juice
1 Vanilla Pod

3 Eggs
1½ oz. Sugar
1 small glass Maraschino
  (Curaçao)

Sprinkle the halved bananas with HONEY and lemon juice. Place in a fireproof dish. Scrape out vanilla pod and divide the centre over the bananas. Separate the egg yolks from the whites and beat the whites to a stiff consistency. Beat up the egg yolks with the sugar and the liqueur and stir in. Pour over the bananas and cook in a medium-hot oven for about ten minutes until light brown. Sprinkle with castor sugar.

Nut-Honey Yogurt

10 grated Hazel Nuts   3 tablespoonsful Honey
Juice of half a Lemon   1 glass Yogurt

Whisk up the grated nuts, HONEY and juice of half
a lemon with the glass of yogurt until it foams.
Serve cold. Delicious!

Curds and Peach Cream

9 oz. Curds   3 tablespoonsful Honey
1 cup White Wine   Halved Peaches
5 tablespoonsful sweet   Fruit to decorate
  Cream   Grated peel of half Lemon

Beat up the curds, wine, cream, lemon peel and
HONEY until well blended. Layer in a dish with the
sugared peach halves. Decorate with peaches and
cherries or strawberries and pistachio nuts.

Dish of the Gods

7 oz. fresh Curds   ⅓ pint Milk
½ vanilla Pod Pulp   1 Egg Yolk
3 tablespoonsful Honey   3½ oz. grated Pumpernickel*
2 oz. Sugar   Bread
Glass of Rum or Arrak   2 oz. grated Chocolate
                           Cherries

Sieve the curds and milk, the pulp of half a vanilla
pod, egg yolk, and HONEY. Then mix together the
pumpernickel bread, sugar and grated chocolate.
Sprinkle with a glass of rum or arrak, and arrange
the curd cream and the breadcrumbs and cherries
in alternate layers in a dish.

* See Appendix.

Grilled Grapefruit

1 Grapefruit   Honey

Halve one grapefruit and prepare in sections. Cover with HONEY and place under the grill. Let the outer peel brown, and serve hot as an hors d'ouvre or as a dessert.

Curds and Honey Nut Cream

1 lb. Cream Curds	Filling:
2 teaspoonsful Sugar	1½ oz. grated Hazel Nuts
2 teaspoonsful Honey	1½ oz. Breadcrumbs
Few drops Vanilla Essence	1 tablespoonful Rum
1 pint Milk	1 tablespoonful Honey
	2 teaspoonsful Wine

Sieve the curds and beat up vigorously with the sugar, HONEY, vanilla essence and milk. Mix all the ingredients for the filling together until well blended. Then layer the curds and nut filling in a small dish and decorate with grated nuts.

Grapes and Curds Dish

9 oz. Cream Curds	Vanilla Sugar
1 glass Yogurt	Ginger Powder
3 tablespoonsful Honey	Grapes
1 small glass Port	

Beat together the curds and the yogurt. Add the HONEY, port, a small quantity of vanilla sugar and a little ginger powder and blend well together. Then stir in halved grapes to taste. Fill glasses with the mixture and decorate with ginger, halved almonds and grapes.

Spanish Pancakes

5 oz. Flour
2 tablespoonsful Sugar
1 small glass Maraschino

1 cup Milk
2 Egg Yolks
2 beaten Egg Whites

Make a pancake mix from the above ingredients. Cook the pancakes in hot fat. Fill with thin HONEY.

Honey Apples

4 large Apples
4 Almonds
4 teaspoonsful Butter
4 teaspoonsful Strawberry
Jam

4 teaspoonsful Honey
1 cup White Wine
Vanilla Sauce

Peel and core the apples without cutting. Close the lower hole with an almond and place in a greased soufflé dish. Fill each apple with one teaspoonful of butter, HONEY and strawberry jam. Pour the wine over the apples and steam gently. Serve with vanilla sauce.

Stockholm Croquants

3 tablespoonsful Honey
1 oz. grated Chocolate
1 teaspoonful Cocoa
1 tablespoonful Butter

1 tablespoonful Sugar
9 oz. grated Almonds
1 pint Cream

Beat together the HONEY, the chocolate and cocoa. Brown the butter, sugar and almonds in a frying pan. Whisk up the cream, add the HONEY and chocolate mixture as well as the fried almonds. Turn into a greased dish and cut into strips when cool.

'Rosé' Nut Dish

4½ oz. grated Walnuts
⅓ pint sweet Cream
2 beaten Egg Whites
1 tablespoonful Sugar
1 leaf Red Gelatine

1 leaf White Gelatine
3 tablespoonful warm Water
2 tablespoonful Honey
1 tablespoonful warm Milk
Pinch of Salt

Mix together the nuts, cream, egg whites and sugar. Dissolve the leaves of gelatine in the warm water and add the HONEY and milk. Season with the salt and beat everything in together. Serve the dish cold and decorate with whipped cream.

Chilian Honey Rice

9 oz. long-grained Rice
1¾ pints Milk
4½ oz. Butter
2½ oz. soaked Raisins

Centre of Vanilla Pod
2½ oz. ground Almonds
2½ oz. Glacé Cherries
5 teaspoonful Honey

Gently boil the rice in the milk and add the butter. Add the raisins, the centre of a vanilla pod, almonds, cherries and HONEY when the rice is cool.

La Dolce Sorpresa

2 heaped tablespoonsful Oats
2 tablespoonsful grated Nuts
5 oz. Apples including peel and core grated

1 cupful Milk
Juice of half a Lemon
1 tablespoonful Raisins
Any other fruit
2-3 tablespoonful Honey

Mix the above ingredients together until well blended, using fruit according to the time of year, and serve at once.

'Victoria' Oat Dish

1 cupful Oats
3 tablespoonsful Honey
1 tablespoonful Orange
  Juice

1 pint Milk
Vanilla Essence

Boil the oats in the milk until the mixture thickens. When cool stir in the HONEY, a little vanilla essence, and the orange juice.

Hobgoblins

3 tablespoonsful ground
  Linseed Seeds
1 pint Milk
2 tablespoonsful Ground
  Nuts

2 tablespoonsful Honey
Juice of 1 Orange
1 grated Apple
Redcurrant Jelly
1 crushed Banana

Bring the milk to the boil and then stir in the linseed seeds. Boil for a short time. Place in a dish to cool. Then stir in the nuts, banana, HONEY, orange juice and apple. Garnish with redcurrant jelly.

Burmese Dumplings

9 oz. Curds
1½ oz. Flour
5 oz. grated Coconut
Sugar Water or Light Wine

Honey
Grated Almonds
Cinnamon or Cocoa

Beat the curds into the flour and coconut. From this mixture form plum-sized dumplings and cook in sugar water or a light wine. When cool, dip in honey and then in grated almonds. Lightly sprinkle with cinnamon or cocoa.

Filled Vine Leaves

Large Vine Leaves
2 oz. chopped Almonds
4 tablespoonsful Honey
2 tablespoonsful Lemon Juice
Olive Oil

5 oz. Rice
3½ oz. caramelled beaten Sugar
1½ oz. Raisins
1 coffeespoonful Cinnamon
Icing Sugar

Wash the vine leaves. Cook the rice and add the chopped almonds, sugar, HONEY, raisins, lemon juice, and cinnamon. Fill the vine leaves with this mixture, roll them up, tie and quickly fry in hot olive oil. Dust with icing sugar.

Honey Pancakes

4 Eggs
3 tablespoonsful Sugar
1½ cupfuls Milk

3 cupfuls Flour
Brandy

Filling:
2 tablespoonsful Honey
1 teaspoonful Vanilla Sugar
1½ oz. sweet grated Almonds
1 coffeespoonful Coffee Powder

3 tablespoonsful Curds
1 cupful sweet Cream
1½ oz. soaked Raisins
1 coffeespoonful Chocolate Powder
Apricot Jam

Mix together the eggs, flour, sugar, a dash of brandy, and the milk to form a thin consistency suitable for pancakes. Fry thin pancakes in hot fat. Spread with a filling made in the following way: beat together the curds, HONEY, sweet cream, and vanilla sugar until smooth. Stir in the raisins, sweet grated almonds, chocolate and coffee powder. Roll up the pancakes and spread with apricot jam.

Fried Honey Apples

| 4 large Apples | 4 knobs Butter |
| A little Honey | Ground Cinnamon |

Core and peel the apples and then place in a
greased frying pan. In the hollow of each apple
place a little HONEY, a knob of butter and some
ground cinnamon. Fry the apples over a moderate
heat—alternatively they can be roasted in the oven.
They ought not to become too soft. Serve with a
vanilla sauce if desired.

Honey Cream with Fruit

⅓-½ pint Cream	2 tablespoonsful Honey
3 tablespoonsful Lemon	Sugared Strawberries
Juice	

Whip the cream with the HONEY until stiff. Add the
lemon juice. Place sugared strawberries (or raspberries) and the HONEY cream in layers in a dish
ending with the HONEY cream. Decorate with
fruits.

Honey Ice Cream

½ pint sweet Cream	1 cupful Honey
½ cupful chopped Dates	½ cupful chopped Figs
¼ cupful Glacé Cherries	¼ cupful chopped Pistachio
	Nuts

Beat up the cream with the HONEY. Stir in the
dates, figs, glacé cherries, and pistachio nuts.
Place in a dish and freeze as a block in the
refrigerator.

CHAPTER XIII

SWEETS

Honey Marshmallows

9 oz. Honey	2 oz. Raisins
1 cup Coconut Oil	2 oz. grated Walnuts
1 cup dry Milk Powder	2 oz. chopped dried Figs
1 pinch Salt	2 oz. skinned dried Apricots
2 oz. dried skinned Plums	

Place the HONEY and oil in a saucepan and add the milk powder and a pinch of salt. Stir the mixture over a moderate heat until it thickens. Then add the fruit and nuts. Stir all the ingredients together and spread in a greased baking tin. When dry, cut into pieces.

Venetian Sweets

4½ oz. sweet Almonds	1 teaspoonful Coconut
6 oz. Castor Sugar	Butter
1 tablespoonful Honey	Assorted Nuts and Cherries
3½ oz. Chocolate	Coloured Sugar

Soak the almonds, skin and dry. Grate and knead to a firm dough with the sugar and HONEY. Shape into rectangles. Mix the chocolate and coconut butter in a saucepan standing in a bowl of hot water and pour over the rectangles. Dot with one almond, walnut, pistachio nut or glacé cherry and sprinkle with coloured sugar.

Honey Kisses

2½ oz. sweet grated
    Almonds
Icing Sugar

1 oz. finely chopped
    Candied Peel
2 teaspoonsful Honey

Mix the almonds with the candied peel and the
HONEY. Make into balls, dip in icing sugar and
stand for two days on greaseproof paper to dry.

Oriental Fruit Rolls

1 lb. 2 oz. Dried Fruits
1 cup grated Walnuts

Honey
Coloured Sugar or
    Chocolate Flakes

Put the dried fruits (e.g. dates, figs, apricots, pears,
sultanas, raisins) through a shredder. Then mix
with the walnuts. Soak in as much honey as the
mixture can hold. Make into a square and press
down over night. Then shape into rolls and dip
into coloured sugar or chocolate flakes.

Tutti-frutti Balls

3 tablespoonsful Honey
2 teaspoonsful Lemon Juice
Candied Peel
Raisins
Finely chopped Ginger

6 tablespoonsful Castor
    Sugar
1 egg cup Rum or Arrak
Glacé Cherries
Quince Jelly
Dessicated Coconut

Blend together the HONEY, sugar, lemon juice and
rum until of a smooth consistency. Stir in the
candied peel, a few cherries and raisins, a little quince
jelly and finely chopped ginger. Shape into balls.
Dip in dessicated coconut or granulated sugar.
Leave to stand for one day to dry.

Lyons Honey Plums

4½ oz. Honey
13½ oz. grated Walnuts
10 drops Rose Water

9 oz. Castor Sugar
Prunes
Cinnamon or Cocoa

Knead together the HONEY, walnuts, rose water and sugar. Shape into walnut-sized balls. In the centre of each ball place a soft prune. Dip in cinnamon or cocoa. These can also be filled with stoned dates.

Grecian Sweets

9 oz. Almonds
2½ oz. Dates
2 Egg Whites

7 oz. Sugar
1 teaspoonful Honey

Peel the almonds and grind. Stone the dates and cut into small pieces. Beat up the egg whites, sugar and HONEY until the mixture foams. Then add the almonds and dates and place in small heaps on rice paper. Cook in a medium-hot oven until golden.

Genoese Honey Jelly

Just under 1 pint Milk
1 tablespoonful white
  Gelatine Powder
3 tablespoonsful Honey

1 tablespoonful Coffee
  Extract
2 tablespoonsful hot Water
Nuts and Jelly Fruits

Heat the milk with the HONEY. Leave to cool. Dissolve the gelatine in the hot water and add the coffee extract. Stir the mixture into the milk. Pour the ready made jelly into a wet baking tin. When it is firm, turn out and decorate with nuts and jelly fruits.

Hazel-nut Honey Balls

2 oz. grated Hazel Nuts
1 oz. grated Chocolate
1½ oz. Sugar
Grated peel of half Lemon

2 tablespoonsful Honey
Vanilla Essence
Chopped Almonds

Stir together the nuts, chocolate, sugar, lemon peel, HONEY and vanilla essence. With damp hands make ten balls from this mixture and dip in finely chopped almonds

Honey Nougat

3 Egg Whites
1 lb. 2 oz. Icing Sugar
9 oz. Honey
5 tablespoonsful Oats

3½ oz. chopped Hazel Nuts
2 oz. chopped Glacé Cherries
2 oz. stoned Dates

Beat together the egg whites, icing sugar, HONEY and oats. Then add the nuts and fruit. Place in a saucepan and stir continuously with a wooden spoon until the mixture thickens. Place on greaseproof paper to cool and cut in pieces with a hot knife.

Almond and Honey Salami

1 lb. 2 oz. Almonds
9 oz. Castor Sugar
2-3 tablespoonsful grated
  Chocolate

3½ oz. Honey
Pinch of grated Nutmeg
Pinch of Cinnamon
Rose Water

Soak the almonds and dry. Mix with the sugar and HONEY. Then add the chocolate. Season with the nutmeg, cinnamon and a little rose water. Make into a thick sausage shape on a sugar-covered board. Roll in greaseproof paper and allow to stand for four days. Then cut.

ALCOHOLIC DRINKS

CHAPTER XIV

ALCOHOLIC DRINKS

Honey Punch

1¾ pints Water   ½ lb. Honey
Cinnamon and Cloves   Thin Orange or Lemon Peel
Juice of Orange or Lemon ⅓ pint good Arrak

Mix together the water, HONEY, a little cinnamon,
a few cloves and the orange or lemon peel and
bring to the boil. Then add the fruit juice and pour
the liquid through a fine muslin into the punch
bowl. Add the arrak. This is enjoyable hot or cold
and can also be bottled. It keeps fresh for several
weeks.

East Fresian Tea Punch

⅓ pint strong Chinese Tea   Brown Barbados Sugar
1 tablespoonful Honey   1 small glass Kümmell

Mix the above ingredients together and drink hot.

Exclusive Honey Cocktail

1 tablespoonful Honey   Juice of 3 Oranges
1 liqueur glass Benedictine
  or Grand Marnier

Mix the above ingredients together and add some
tiny ice cubes.

'Fiaker' Cognac Milk

⅓ pint Milk
1 section Lemon Peel
2 Egg Yolks

2 tablespoonful Honey
3 tablespoonsful Cognac

Place the lemon peel in the milk and bring to the boil. Then strain the liquid through a sieve. Beat the egg yolks with the HONEY and carefully blend into the warm milk. Add the cognac.

'Bellevue' Fruit Drink

⅓ pint Orange Juice
2 tablespoonsful Lemon Juice
1 cup cold Water
1 teaspoonful finely chopped Nuts
1 tablespoonful Honey

⅓ pint Grapefruit Juice
1½ tablespoonsful chopped Lemon Peel
6 whole Cloves
1 teaspoonful Sugar
1 slice Candied Ginger
Ice-cold Beer

Mix together the fruit juices, lemon peel, cold water, cloves, nuts, sugar and HONEY. Leave to stand for two hours in a warm place. Then add the candied ginger and fill with the beer.

Toddy

Whisky
1 dessertspoonful Honey

Lemon Juice

Mix whisky with hot water according to taste. Add sugar if wanted, a little lemon juice and the honey. Serve hot.

CHAPTER XV

HONEY IN COSMETICS

In former times people knew that honey not only worked marvels internally but could also be used externally with benefit. This advice was found in an old Egyptian medicine book of the doctor, Papyr Eber: place a piece of linen in incense and honey, in order that the wounds might heal more quickly. The great Grecian doctor, Hippocrates, 400 B.C., recommended a mixture of honey and salt to clear up ulcers. Pliny, a contemporary of Jesus Christ, prescribed honey as a remedy for mouth ulcers and quinsy. Dioskorides, a doctor who lived in A.D. 50 wrote: "Honey has cleaning and opening powers and can draw out the humours." For that reason it is suitable for pouring on dirty ulcers and fistulas. When boiled and applied to separate parts of the body, it can be used to dress wounds. When boiled with alum and rubbed in, it heals dry scabs and ear-ache and, if the honey is sprinkled with finely ground rock salt, it can cure a sensation of ringing in the ears. It prevents the darkening of the pupils and is more effective in healing larynx, tonsil and pharynx infections than mouth washes and gargles.

Modern beautycare values the vital ingredients in honey most highly. Honey is used on the skin in the form of face packs and ointments and can make one feel years younger. The enzymes in honey are especially effective when the ointment is applied slightly warm. The honey face pack can be used to treat the face, neck and upper part of the chest. It should be left for fifteen minutes on the body and then washed off with warm water. As a result of these masks the skin is restored to its natural beauty.

Tips for applying and using Honey

Honey as an internal beauty agent—take two tablespoonsful of honey every morning on an empty stomach. It contains almost all the important salts and minerals and provides, moreover, a means of purifying the blood.

Make a honey cream to refresh and smooth rough, blemished skin; beat two tablespoonful of liquid honey, one egg yolk and one dessertspoonsful of sweet cream together until of a thick consistency. Place on the face and leave for twenty minutes. Then wash off with lime-blossom tea.

To treat freckles, brown spots and wrinkles: stir crushed fennel seeds into warm, thin liquid honey until of a thick consistency. Spread on the face and leave for fifteen minutes. Wash off with chicory water. The skin is then clean and rosy.

Mayonnaise for the complexion: beat one dessertspoonful of freshly beaten linseed oil with one egg yolk. Add one coffee-spoonful of honey. Spread on the skin with a soft brush and leave for fifteen minutes. Wash off with rose water.

Liquid honey to make the hair grow: make up a liquid from honey and distilled water in the ratio of one to six and daily massage well into the scalp. This keeps the hair fresh and prevents it falling out.

Skin discolouration: this can be remedied by a mixture of honey and the juice of watercress. Spread on the face, leave to dry and wash off after one to two hours. Renew the compress daily.

Honey compress for tired eyes: bring to the boil eyebright mixed with half tablespoonful of honey. Soak small pieces of linen in this mixture and place for thirty minutes on the closed eyes.

APPENDIX

Potato flour—this is used far more on the continent as a thickening agent. Cornflour can be substituted.

Recipe: Peel and wash some floury potatoes and grate them into a large pan of cold water. Stir well and strain through a sieve and then let the grated potato settle till the water is quite clear. Pour off the water, add more fresh and stir well. Let the potato settle and leave for ten minutes. Repeat till the water is clear and the powder settled at the bottom of the pan is fine and pure white. Then spread the sediment to dry on large dishes in front of a fire or in the sun. Turn very frequently and pound well. Rub through a hair sieve and store in tightly corked jars.

Rye flour—this is used a great deal on the continent to make so-called " Black" bread. A brown flour can be substituted and this is especially advisable for those interested in diet reform.

Pumpernickel—this is a black bread from Germany. If not available, wholemeal bread should be used.

N.B.   The regional names of certain dishes have been retained, where the dish originated in that locality.

INDEX

119

OWN RECIPES

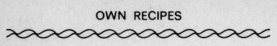

OWN RECIPES

OWN RECIPES

OWN RECIPES

Ancient wisdom is often ahead of modern science! These two *Nature's Way* titles provide fascinating insights into such wisdom.

COLOUR HEALING

Chromotherapy and How It Works

Mary Anderson

'Seeing red', 'feeling blue', 'green with jealousy', 'black with rage', all relate to actual changes which take place in the colours of our body's electromagnetic field due to changes in the emotions. Psychologically we are all affected by colour, and rays from coloured lamps can be applied to diseased organs with amazingly beneficial results. This book reveals the complete therapy.

THE INCREDIBLE HEALING NEEDLES

A Layman's Guide to Chinese Acupuncture

Denis Lawson-Wood F.Ac.A. & Joyce Lawson-Wood

Following world-wide press and TV coverage of surgical operations being performed in China with acupuncture replacing conventional anaesthetics, the authors answer questions many laymen are asking: What is acupuncture? How does it work? Will it cure me? Acupuncture is at least five thousand years old — indicating that the ancients possessed knowledge and investigation techniques far superior to anything yet attained by western science.

Valuable additions to the ABOUT library of health.

ABOUT COMFREY
The Forgotten Herb

Reveals the many uses of a herb rich in minerals and vitamins and provides notes on cultivation, with a selection of comfrey recipes. The book also features borage, another excellent herb in the same plant family.

ABOUT YOGA DIET
The Eastern Way to Healthy Eating

How to recapture the vegetarian vigour which characterized the peoples of ancient India; with advice on the use of herbs and recipes for preparing really tasty and nutritious meatless dishes.

ABOUT POLLEN
Health Food and Healing Agent

A fascinating survey of the richest source yet revealed of vitamins, minerals, proteins, amino acids, hormones, enzymes and fats. Author demonstrates how pollen, essential for all plant life and garnered by bees, is a perfect food and medicine.

ABOUT DIET FOR DIABETICS
How Natural Foods Can Help

Explains the causes and symptoms of diabetes; how diabetics can be restored to good health by eating certain foods and avoiding others; with details of proven specimen meals devised by Dr Valentine Knaggs.

ABOUT WHEAT GERM
Nature's Source of Vital Vitamins

Explains the wheat germ's composition and place in our dietary; its importance in terms of vitamins A, E and the B-complex; and the threat posed by its removal from our daily bread by modern milling processes.

Other books for better health the natural way.

THE VITAMINS EXPLAINED SIMPLY

Vitamins are chemical compounds which, with minor exceptions, cannot be made in the body, but come from food. Without vitamins neither normal development nor health is possible. Last century food contained all man's nutritional requirements; today the vitamin content of food is dangerously diminished by processing and chemical additives. This book reveals what ailments vitamins prevent and remedy and gives estimated daily requirements of each vitamin.

IMPROVE YOUR SIGHT WITHOUT GLASSES

Demolishes a long-cherished belief that the only remedy for refractory eye troubles is spectacles. In fact this book demonstrates that eye troubles can be eliminated and sight tremendously improved by a simple combination of exercises and dietary measures, without using spectacles — which are merely 'crutches'. Also gives treatment for cataract, conjunctivitis and glaucoma, and explains hyperimetropia (far sight) and myopia (short sight).

RHEUMATISM AND ARTHRITIS

Explains the main rheumatic categories of rheumatoid arthritis, osteo-arthritis, lumbago, neuritis, sciatica, gout, spondylitis, bursitis and rheumatic fever; causes of rheumatic ailments; the injurious side effects of orthodox therapies; with advice on applying natural remedial principles and the sweat therapy. Gives hope to all rheumatic and arthritic sufferers.

EATING FOR HEALTH

Reveals the hard truth that indiscriminate eating leads to poor health and disease. Invaluable advice on balanced diet, acid and alkaline foods, protein and amino acids, vitamins and minerals. Also exposes the fallacious calorie standard and dishonest propaganda for white bread and flour. With alphabetical list of foods and pithy comments on each item's dietary value or harmful properties.

FIT FOR ANYTHING
Exercising Your Muscles and Joints for All-round Health and Fitness
Keki R. Sidhwa N.D., D.O.

How to exercise joints and muscles to combat 'diseases of civilization'. Gives a 'daily dozen' routine for building up strength and stamina, and includes a wide range of corrective movements for specific physical and postural weaknesses.

MOLASSES AND NUTRITION
Alan Moyle, N.D., M.B.N.O.A.

Explains the nutritional significance of molasses and its value in treating many disorders, including constipation, intestinal troubles and rheumatism; with an account of sugar cane harvesting and a varied selection of molasses recipes for laxative mixtures, muesli, puddings, cakes, jellies and scones.

HERBS FOR RHEUMATISM AND ARTHRITIS
Sarah Beckett

Describes twenty-five herbs for treating rheumatism and arthritis by ridding the body of excess acids and purifying the blood. With supplementary advice on dietetics, vitamins, Epsom salts baths and compresses, exercise and relaxation.

ARTHRITIS
Help In Your Own Hands
Helen B. MacFarlane

The story of one woman's successful fight against crippling arthritis, and how she regained full use of her limbs by a combination of diet, special exercises and massage. With notes on aids and appliances available for all arthritis sufferers.